ICKY ANIMALS! Small and Gross

SCRAMBLING SPIDERS

Celeste Bishop

PowerKiDS press.

New York

Published in 2016 by The Rosen Publishing Group, Inc.
29 East 21st Street, New York, NY 10010

First Edition

Editor: Sarah Machajewski
Book Design: Mickey Harmon

Photo Credits: Cover (spider) EBPhoto/Shutterstock.com; cover, pp. 1, 3–4, 7–8, 11–12, 15–16, 19–20, 23–24 (splatters) GreenBelka/Shutterstock.com; p. 5 Kirsanov Valeriy Vladimirovich/Shutterstock.com; p. 6 SARIN KUNTHONG/Shutterstock.com; p. 9 Paul Looyen/Shutterstock.com; p. 10 89Studio/Shutterstock.com; p. 13 John Mitchell/Science Source/Getty Images; p. 14 Dr. Morley Read/Shutterstock.com; p. 17 Dirk Ercken/Shutterstock.com; pp. 18, 24 (web) Ian Grainger/Shutterstock.com; p. 21 Matteo photos/Shutterstock.com; p. 22 Benjamin F. Haith/Shutterstock.com; p. 24 (hand) Tania Zbrodko/Shutterstock.com.

Library of Congress Cataloging-in-Publication Data

Bishop, Celeste, author.
Scrambling spiders / Celeste Bishop.
pages cm. — (Icky animals! Small and gross)
Includes index.
ISBN 978-1-4994-0717-4 (pbk.)
ISBN 978-1-4994-0718-1 (6 pack)
ISBN 978-1-4994-0719-8 (library binding)
1. Spiders—Juvenile literature. I. Title. II. Series: Bishop, Celeste. Icky animals! Small and gross.
QL458.4.B577 2015
595.4'4—dc23

2014048527

Manufactured in the United States of America

CPSIA Compliance Information: Batch #WS15PK: For Further Information contact Rosen Publishing, New York, New York at 1-800-237-9932

CONTENTS

There are many kinds of spiders.
They live all over the world.

How do you know if a bug is a spider? Count its legs. All spiders have eight legs.

Spiders can have up to eight eyes. Most spiders can't see well.

Spiders can be many colors and sizes. Some spiders are smaller than a **fingernail**.

The Goliath bird-eating spider is the biggest spider in the world.

Spiders eat other animals.
Most eat bugs.

Some spiders are big enough to eat frogs and birds!

Some spiders make **webs** to catch their food. Spider webs are very sticky.

Spiders may bite if they feel scared. The black widow spider is known for its painful bite.

If you ever see a spider, don't be afraid! Most of them don't hurt people.

WORDS TO KNOW

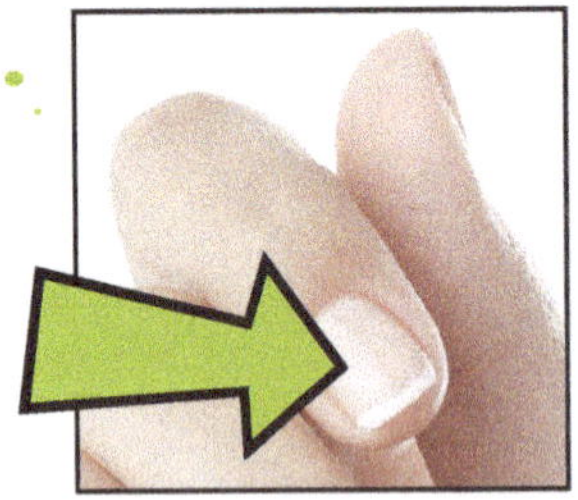

fingernail

web

INDEX

WEBSITES

Due to the changing nature of Internet links, PowerKids Press has developed an online list of websites related to the subject of this book. This site is updated regularly. Please use this link to access the list: www.powerkidspress.com/icky/spdr